SOMETIMES I'M AFRAID

A Read-Together Book for Parents & Children

Sometimes I'm Afraid

by Jane Werner Watson

Robert E. Switzer, M.D.
Former Director of the Children's Division
The Menninger Clinic

J. Cotter Hirschberg, M.D.
William C. Menninger Distinguished Professor of Psychiatry
The Menninger Clinic

with pictures by Irene Trivas

Crown Publishers, Inc.   New York

A Read-Together Book for Parents and Children™
Created in cooperation with the Menninger Foundation

The Dorothy Wright Treatment and Endowment Fund defrays a part of the care
and treatment cost at the Children's Division
of the Menninger Clinic, Box 829, Topeka, Kansas 66601.
Part of the income from the sale of this book goes to that fund.

Library of Congress Cataloging-in-Publication Data Watson, Jane Werner, 1915– Sometimes I'm afraid. (A Read-together book for parents and children) Summary: A three-year-old describes some of the things he is afraid of and how his parents help quiet his fears. 1. Fear—Juvenile literature. [1. Fear] I. Switzer, Robert E., 1918– . II. Hirschberg, J. Cotter, 1915– . III. Trivas, Irene, ill. IV. Title. V. Series. BF723.F4W38 1986 155.42'3 85-24252
ISBN 0-517-56087-9
10 9 8 7 6 5 4 3 2 1
First Edition

NOTE TO PARENTS

No matter how eager we may be to make childhood a completely happy experience for our children, we must face the fact that there will be moments of fear and anxiety for them as well as those of pleasure and satisfaction. If we as parents recognize the kinds of situations, both real and imaginary, both within the child himself* and out in his big, ever-growing world, that cause him to be afraid, we can help to minimize and soothe away the moments of fear.

It is especially important for us to realize how much our reactions affect the child's feelings. If we become upset when the

---

*The authors use "*he*," "*him*," and "*his*" for simplicity instead of the somewhat awkward "*he or she*," "*his or her*," and "*him or her*," but with no suggestion of preference implied.

child does not feel well or is constipated, has a lapse in his toilet training or gives way to a temper tantrum, we increase the youngster's sense of failure, of wrongdoing, his sense of shame and fear. To the extent that we remain calm and cheerful and can accept and explain the situation as regrettable and to be avoided when possible but a natural part of growing up, we lessen the child's fear and reinforce his feeling of his own worth.

Every child is fearful of being left out of the family circle of affection, of being disliked and rejected, of being made to feel bad and worthless. Even if he has genuinely—and apparently intentionally—done wrong, the tantrum or other misdeed should be calmly though firmly and promptly dealt with. If the child is put into his own room to "cool off," he should be made to understand that he will be warmly welcomed back as soon as he has gotten rid of his anger.

If a child's fear has an external cause, such as wind or storm or sudden loud noise, the comfort of being held and reassured will do wonders to still it. If Mommy or Daddy has carried with her or him from childhood an unresolved fear— of lightning and thunder, of the dark, of dogs or cats, or of going into the water—it is of course more difficult to keep from passing this onto children. But it is worth a good deal of effort on the parents' part to avoid letting children "catch" a chronic, unreasonable fear from them.[†]

Fearlessness should not, of course, be carried to the point of disregarding safety precautions. As soon as the child learns the meaning of *no* he should be taught safety patterns such as staying away from cars and streets unless an adult is escorting him, and so on. The more he understands his fears, reasonable and unreasonable alike, and the limits within which he is expected to operate, the more comfortable and happy he will be.

New experiences for which we do not feel prepared are likely to be unsettling, for us as adults and more so for young children. The more we can prepare children for new happenings, the less upset they will be by them. A new baby-sitter should be introduced before the parents leave. A new day-care center should be visited and discussed before the child is left there

---

[†]The distress caused to a young child by awareness of discord between his parents can scarcely be overemphasized. His secure world becomes threatened when he hears his parents' voices raised in anger.

for the first time. Visits to the doctor should be explained; and if there is going to be a moment that hurts a little, the child should be prepared for it so that he will not feel shock and mistrust. Not too many new people should be introduced into the child's world at one time; they are likely to be frightening just because they are new. Nor should the child be hurried beyond a comfortable pace for him at his learning processes. His feeling of satisfaction and mastery in an accomplishment, however slow, is much more important than the accomplishment itself.

We hope the child will not be exposed to frightening programs on television, for it is difficult for him to separate the imaginary from the real. If he is upset by make-believe or imaginary terrors, these should not be ridiculed. The child should be encouraged to talk about his fear and be reassured warmly by his parent. If the fear continues to trouble him, he may want to talk about it more than once.

It is important to remember that most fears, at any age, grow when they are locked away, and shrivel when brought out into daylight and talked about, quietly and calmly. We hope that reading this book, or relevant parts of it, together will provide background for helpful discussions with your child. Encourage him to ask questions about things that puzzle—and perhaps frighten—him. Provide simple, direct answers, as factual as you can manage. As you reinforce your child's feeling of being comfortable and self-confident in a widening world, chances are that you will find your own fears dwindling too.

ROBERT E. SWITZER, M.D.
Former Director of the Children's Division
The Menninger Clinic

J. COTTER HIRSCHBERG, M.D.
William C. Menninger Distinguished Professor of Psychiatry
The Menninger Clinic

I am three, and you can see
I have learned a lot
being one, two, three.

Still, when things are strange or new
and I don't know just what to do
sometimes I feel afraid.
Do you?

If my parents are suddenly gone—
maybe far away—
and I can't go with them
and everyone around seems strange to me,
then I feel afraid.

New people and places
and things I don't understand
scare me a little.

When I get to know
people I meet
and new places we go

I like them fine.
And I'm learning more new things
all the time.

Sometimes loud noises scare me,
or creaks in the dark of night,
or shadows that look
like monsters or ghosts
when there is no light.

Then having Mommy or Daddy
hold me close
makes me feel good inside.
Or they turn on the light
and let me see
there is nothing hiding to frighten me.

Sometimes there's scary make-believe
in a movie or television play.
If I talk it over
with Mommy or Daddy
the scariness goes away.

Sometimes I have dreams
so scary
they wake me up with a start.
If I tell Mommy or Daddy about them,
just talking takes away the scary part.

Mommy and Daddy explain things,
like how lightning and thunder
happen up in the clouds of rain.

I ask a lot of questions
and as soon as they explain
how things work
and what they mean,
those things don't scare me.

Oh, noisy streets and car horns
and squealing brakes are scary.
Mommy and Daddy say
being a little afraid
of real dangers like those
is necessary.
Then you remember
to be careful.

Sometimes I'm afraid
of big dogs and cats
and other animals.
My parents say,
"It's just as well
to keep a little distance away
from strange animals.
They may not understand
that you want to play."

And they show me how to play
nicely with pets I know,
so I will not hurt them
without meaning to.

That is true with children too.
Mostly I give other children
a turn when we play
together
and don't cry or get angry
when I don't have my way.

Sometimes I get stubborn
to let people know
that having my way
is important too.
But if I'm really so angry
that I feel bad inside
and want to hurt someone,

my parents let me stay
in my room by myself
for a while
to "cool off."
Then the scary feeling
that being angry gives me
goes away.

But mostly I know
how much better I feel
if I just don't do things
that make people
unhappy with me.

When Mommy and Daddy
are pleased with me,
I feel warm and happy
as I can be.

If Mommy and Daddy are unhappy
and shout and argue or fight,
I get so scared
I don't know what to do.

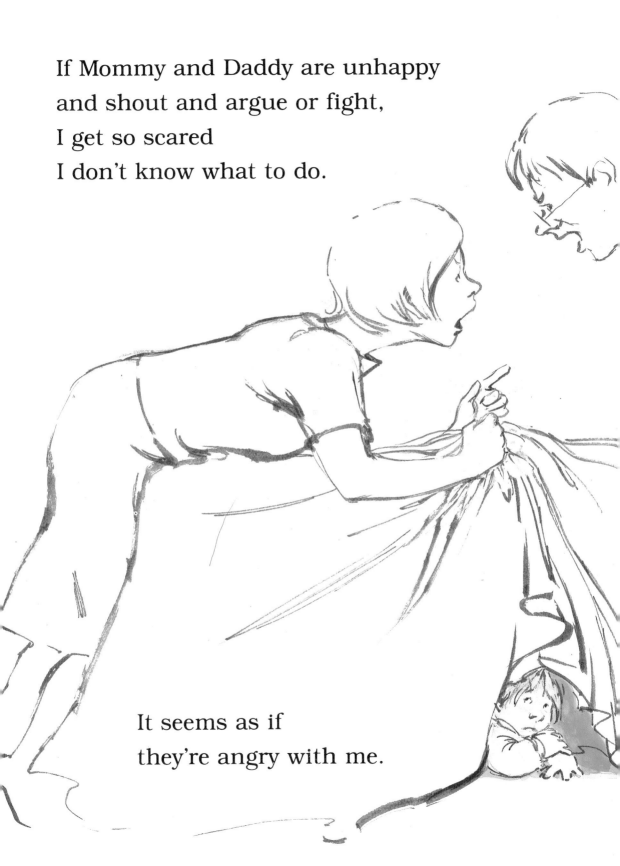

It seems as if
they're angry with me.

I feel scared most of all
of things I don't understand.
Sometimes I don't understand
how my body works.

If I get sick
and my tummy feels strange,
I'm afraid I may vomit.
Or I'm afraid I may have an accident.
Or if I have a hard b.m.,
it scares me.

If Mommy explains it to me
and I feel that she's not afraid,
it doesn't seem so bad.
But if Mommy gets upset too,
I catch more fear from her.

We talk about things
like going to the doctor
and letting him take
a little bit of blood to test,
or letting him prick my arm
to keep me from
getting sick.

It might hurt for a minute,
but I'm not scared,
because I understand.

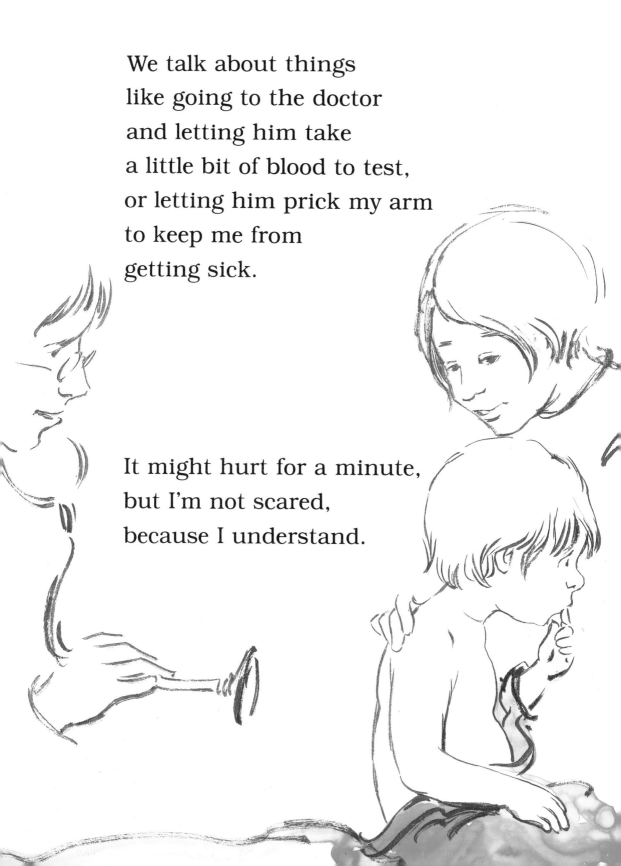

We talk about going to the dentist
to help keep my teeth strong,
and about how police
and fire fighters
help keep us safe.

I play being doctor
and fireman,
and it's fun.
Maybe I'll grow up to be one
someday.

Sometimes I'm afraid
to try to do
things that are new.
But if I don't do a thing right
the first time,
Mommy and Daddy
don't mind.
They help me to try and try
until I learn how, by and by.

Whenever I learn something new
they are so pleased!
And everything I learn to do
means I'm less afraid
of the whole world, too.

Mommy and Daddy understand
how it feels
to be afraid
sometimes.

Knowing they love me
and are near
to help me
takes away my fear,
and makes me feel good and safe.